The Story of General

Jean Lang

Alpha Editions

This edition published in 2024

ISBN : 9789362925749

Design and Setting By
Alpha Editions
www.alphaedis.com
Email - info@alphaedis.com

As per information held with us this book is in Public Domain.
This book is a reproduction of an important historical work. Alpha Editions uses the best technology to reproduce historical work in the same manner it was first published to preserve its original nature. Any marks or number seen are left intentionally to preserve its true form.

Contents

PREFACE ....- 1 -

CHAPTER I "CHARLIE GORDON" ....- 2 -

CHAPTER II GORDON'S FIRST BATTLES ....- 8 -

CHAPTER III "CHINESE GORDON"..- 14 -

CHAPTER IV THE "KERNEL" ....- 28 -

CHAPTER V GORDON AND THE SLAVERS..- 34 -

CHAPTER VI KHARTOUM ....- 48 -

PREFACE

DEAR ARCHIE AND BERTIE,

When boys read the old fairy tales, and the stories of King Arthur's Round Table, and the Knights of the Faerie Queen, they sometimes wonder sadly why the knights that they see are not like those of the olden days.

Knights now are often stout old gentlemen who never rode horses or had lances in their hands, but who made much money in the City, and who have no more furious monsters near them than their own motor-cars.

Only a very few knights are like what your own grandfather was.

"I wish I had lived long ago," say some of the boys. "Then I might have killed dragons, and fought for my Queen, and sought for the Holy Grail. Nobody does those things now. Though I can be a soldier and fight for the King, that is a quite different thing."

But if the boys think this, it is because they do not quite understand.

Even now there live knights as pure as Sir Galahad, as brave and true as St. George. They may not be what the world calls "knights"; yet they are fighting against all that is not good, and true, and honest, and clean, just as bravely as the knights fought in days of old.

And it is of one of those heroes, who sought all his life to find what was holy, who fought all his life against evil, and who died serving his God, his country, and his Queen, that I want to tell you now.

Your friend,
    JEANIE LANG.

CHAPTER I
"CHARLIE GORDON"

Sixty years ago, at Woolwich, the town on the Thames where the gunners of our army are trained, there lived a mischievous, curly-haired, blue-eyed boy, whose name was Charlie Gordon.

The Gordons were a Scotch family, and Charlie came of a race of soldiers. His great-grandfather had fought for King George, and was taken prisoner at the battle of Prestonpans, when many other Gordons were fighting for Prince Charlie. His grandfather had served bravely in different regiments and in many lands. His father was yet another gallant soldier, who thought that there was no life so good as the soldier's life, and nothing so fine as to serve in the British army. Of him it is said that he was "kind-hearted, generous, cheerful, full of humour, always just, living by the code of honour," and "greatly beloved." His wife belonged to a family of great merchant adventurers and explorers, the Enderbys, whose ships had done many daring things on far seas.

Charlie Gordon's mother was one of the people who never lose their tempers, who always make the best of everything, and who are always thinking of how to help others and never of themselves.

So little Charlie came of brave and good people, and when he was a very little boy he must have heard much of his soldier uncles and cousins and his soldier brother, and must even have seen the swinging kilts and heard the pipes of the gallant regiment that is known as the Gordon Highlanders.

Charles George Gordon was born at Woolwich on the 28th January 1833, but while he was still a little child his father, General Gordon, went to hold a command in Corfu, an island off the coast of Turkey, at the mouth of the Adriatic Sea. The Duke of Cambridge long afterwards spoke of the bright little boy who used to be in the room next his in that house in Corfu, but we know little of Charles Gordon until he was ten years old. His father was then given an important post at Woolwich, and he and his family returned to England.

Then began merry days for little Charlie.

In long after years he wrote to one of his nieces about the great building at Woolwich where firearms for the British army are made and stored: "You never, any of you, made a proper use of the Arsenal workmen, as we did. They used to neglect their work for our orders, and turned out some splendid squirts—articles that would wet you through in a minute. As for the cross-bows they made, they were grand with screws."

There were five boys and six girls in the Gordon family. Charlie was the fourth son, and two of his elder brothers were soldiers while he was still quite a little lad.

It was in his holidays that the Arsenal was his playground, for on the return from Corfu he was sent to school at Taunton, where you may still see his initials, "C.G.G.", carved deep on the desk he used.

At school he did not seem to be specially clever. He was not fond of lessons, but he drew very well, and made first-rate maps. He was always brimful of high spirits and mischief, and ready for any sort of sport, and the people of Woolwich must have sighed when Charlie came home for his holidays.

One time when he came he found that his father's house was overrun with mice. This was too good a chance to miss. He and one of his brothers caught all the mice they could, carried them to the house of the commandant of the garrison, which was opposite to theirs, gently opened the door, and let the mice loose in their new home.

Once, with the screw-firing cross-bows that the workmen at the Arsenal had made for them, the wild Gordon boys broke twenty-seven panes of glass in one of the large warehouses of the Arsenal. A captain who was in the room narrowly escaped being shot, one of the screws passing close to his head and fixing itself into the wall as if it had been placed there by a screwdriver.

Freddy, the youngest of the five boys, had an anxious, if merry, time when his big brothers came back from school. With them he would ring the doorbells of houses till the angry servants of Woolwich seemed for ever to be opening doors to invisible ringers. Often, too, little Freddy would be pushed into a house, the bell rung by his mischievous brothers, and the door held, so that Freddy alone had to face the surprised people inside.

But the wildest of their tricks was one that they played on the cadets at Woolwich—the big boys who were being trained to be officers of artillery. "The Pussies" was the name they went by, and it was on the most grown up of the Pussies that they directed their mischief. The senior class of cadets was then stationed in the Royal Arsenal, in front of which were earthworks on which they learned how to defend and fortify places in time of war. All the ins and outs of these earthworks were known to Charlie Gordon and his brothers. One dark night, when a colonel was lecturing to the cadets, a crash as of a fearful explosion was heard. The cadets, thinking that every pane of glass in the lecture hall was broken, rushed out like bees from a hive. They soon saw that the terrific noise had been made by round shot being thrown at the windows, and well they knew that Charlie Gordon was sure to be at the bottom of the trick. But the night was dark, and Charlie knew every passage of the earthworks better than any big cadet there. Although there were many big boys as hounds and only two little boys as hares, the Gordons easily escaped from the angry cadets. For some time afterwards they carefully kept away from the Arsenal, for they knew that if the "Pussies" should catch them they need expect no mercy.

From Taunton Charlie went for one year to be coached for the army at a school at Shooters Hill. From there, when he was not quite sixteen, he passed into the Royal Military Academy at Woolwich.

As a cadet, Charlie Gordon was no more of a book-worm than he had been as a schoolboy. There was no piece of mischief, no wild prank, that that boy with the curly fair hair and merry blue eyes did not have a share in. But if he fairly shared the fun, Charlie would sometimes take more than his fair share of blame or punishment. He was never afraid to own up, and he was always ready to bear his friends' punishment as well as his own for scrapes they had got into together. Of course he got into scrapes. There was never a boy that was full of wild spirits who did not. But Charlie Gordon never got into a scrape for any thoughtless mischief and naughtiness. He never did anything mean, never anything that was not straight, and true, and honourable.

He had been at the Academy for some time, and had earned many good-conduct badges, when complaint was made of the noise and roughness with which the cadets rushed down the narrow staircase from their dining-room. One of the senior cadets, a corporal, was stationed at the head of this staircase, his arms outstretched, to prevent the usual wild rush past. The sight of this severe little officer was too great a temptation for Charlie Gordon. Down went his head, forward he rushed, and the corporal was butted not only downstairs, but right through the glass door beyond. The corporal's body escaped unhurt, but his feelings did not, and Charlie was placed under arrest, and very nearly expelled from the College.

The Corporal was butted downstairs

When his term at Woolwich was nearly over, a great deal of bullying was found to be going on, and the new boys were questioned about it by the officers in charge. One new boy said that Charlie Gordon had hit him on the head with a clothes-brush—"not a severe blow," he had to own. But Charlie's bear-fighting had this time a hard punishment, for he was put back six months for his commission.

Until then he had meant to be an officer of Artillery—a "gunner," as they are called. Now he knew that he would always be six months behind his gunner friends, and so decided to work instead for the Engineers, and get his commission as a "sapper."

At college, as well as at school, his map-drawing was very good, and his mother was very proud of what he did. One day he found her showing some visitors a map he had made. His hatred of being praised for what he thought he did not deserve, and his hot temper, sprang out together, and he tore up the map and threw it in the grate.

But almost at once he was sorry for his rudeness and unkindness, and afterwards he carefully pasted the torn pieces of the map together for his mother.

"How my mother loved me!" he wrote of her long years afterwards.

His hot temper was sometimes shown to his officers. He would bear more than his share of blame when he felt that he deserved it, but when he felt that blame was undeserved, his temper would flash out in a sudden storm.

One of his superiors at Woolwich once said, scolding him,—"You will never make an officer."

Charlie's honour was touched. His temper blazed out, and he tore off his epaulettes and threw them at the officer's feet.

He always hated his examinations, yet he never failed to pass them.

When he was fifty years old, he wrote to his sister,—"I had a fearful dream last night: I was back at the Academy, and had to pass an examination! I was wide awake enough to know I had forgotten all I had ever learnt, and it was truly some time ere I could collect myself and realise I was a general, so completely had I become a cadet again. What misery those examinations were!"

When he was nineteen, Charlie Gordon became Sub-Lieutenant Charles Gordon of the Royal Engineers.

From Woolwich he went to Chatham, the headquarters of the Royal Engineers, to have some special training as an Engineer officer.

There he found his cleverness at map-drawing a great help in his work, and for nearly two years he worked hard at all that an officer of Engineers must know, and soon he was looked on as a very promising young officer.

In February 1854, he gained the rank of full lieutenant, and was sent to Pembroke Dock to help with the new fortifications and batteries that were being made there.

Whatever Charlie Gordon did, he did with all his might, and he was now as keen on making plans and building fortifications, as he had once been in planning and playing mischievous tricks.

When he returned to Pembroke thirty years later, an old ferryman there remembered him.

"Are you the gent who used to walk across the stream right through the water?" he asked.

And all through his life no stream was too strong for Gordon to face.

Gordon had not been long at Pembroke when a great war broke out between Russia on one side, and England, France, and Turkey on the other. It was fought in a part of Russia called the Crimea, and is known as the Crimean War.

The two elder Gordons, Henry and Enderby, were out there with their batteries, and, like every other keen young soldier, Charlie Gordon was wild to go.

After a few months at Pembroke, orders came for him to go to Corfu. He suspected his father of having managed to get him sent there to be out of harm's way.

"It is a great shame of you," he wrote. But very shortly afterwards came fresh orders, telling him to go to the Crimea without delay.

A general whom he had told how much he longed to go where the fighting was, had had the orders changed.

On the 4th December 1854 his orders came to Pembroke. Two days later he reported himself at the War Office in London, and on the evening of the same day he was at Portsmouth, ready to sail. At first it was intended that he should go out in a collier, but that arrangement was altered. Back he came to London, and went from there to France.

At Marseilles he got a ship to Constantinople, and just as fearlessly and as happily as he had ever gone on one of his mischievous expeditions as a little boy, Charlie Gordon went off to face hardships, and dangers, and death in the Crimea, and to learn his first lessons in war.

CHAPTER II
GORDON'S FIRST BATTLES

The Crimean War had been going on for several months when, on New Year's Day 1855, Gordon reached Balaclava.

The months had been dreary ones for the English soldiers, for, through bad management in England, they had had to face a bitter Russian winter, and go through much hard fighting, without proper food, without warm clothing, and with no proper shelter.

Night after night, and day after day, in pitilessly falling snow, or in drenching rain, clad in uniforms that had become mere rags, cold and hungry, tired and wet, the English soldiers had to line the trenches before Sebastopol.

These trenches were deep ditches, with the earth thrown up to protect the men who fired from them, and in them the men often had to stand hour after hour, knee deep in mud, and in cold that froze the blood in their veins.

Illness broke out in the camp, and many men died from cholera. Many had no better bed than leaves spread on stones in the open could give them.

Some of those who had tents, and used little charcoal fires to warm them, were killed by the fumes of charcoal.

A "Black Winter" it was called, and the Black Winter was not over when Gordon arrived. He had been sent out in charge of 320 huts, which had followed him in the collier from Portsmouth, so that now, at least, some of the men were better sheltered than they had been before. But they were still half-starved, and in very low spirits. Officers and men had constantly to go foraging for food, or else to go hungry, and men died every day of the bitter cold. And all the time the guns of the Russians were never idle.

It was not a very gay beginning for a young officer's active service, but Gordon, like his mother, had a way of making the best of things. Even when, as he wrote, the ink was frozen, and he broke the nib of his pen as he dipped it, "There are really no hardships for the officers," he wrote home; "the men are the sufferers."

Before he had been a month out, Gordon was put on duty in the trenches before Sebastopol, a great fortified town by the sea.

On the night of 14th February, with eight men with picks and shovels, and five double sentries, he was sent to make a connection between the French and English outposts by means of rifle-pits. It was a pitch black night, and as yet Gordon did not know the trenches as well as he had known the earthworks at Woolwich Arsenal. He led his men, and, missing his way, nearly walked into the town filled with Russians. Turning back, they crept up the trenches to some caves which the English should have held, but found no sentries there. Taking one man with him, Gordon explored the caves. He feared that the Russians, finding them undefended, might have taken possession of them when darkness fell, but he found them empty. He then posted two sentries on the hill above the caves, and went back to post two others down below. No sooner did he and these two appear below than "Bang! bang!" went two rifles, and the bullets ripped up the ground at Gordon's feet. Off rushed the two men who were with him, and off scampered the eight sappers, thinking that the whole Russian army was at their heels. But all that had really happened was that the sentries on the hill above, seeing Gordon and his men coming stealthily out of the caves in the darkness, had taken them for Russians, and fired straight at them. The mischief did not end there. A Russian picket was stationed only 150 yards away, and the sound of the shots made them also send a shower of bullets, one of which hit a man on the breast, passed through his coats, grazed his ribs, and passed out again without hurting him. But no serious harm was done, and by working all night Gordon and his men carried out their orders.

It was not long before Gordon learned so thoroughly all the ins and outs of the trenches that the darkest night made no difference to him. "Come with me after dark, and I will show you over the trenches," he said to a friend who had been away on sick leave, and who complained to him that he could not find his way about. "He drew me a very clear sketch of the lines," writes his friend, Sir Charles Stavely, "explained every nook and corner, and took me along outside our most advanced trench, the bouquets (volleys of small shells fired from mortars) and other missiles flying about us in, to me, a very unpleasant manner, he taking the matter remarkably coolly."

Before many weeks were past, Gordon not only knew the trenches as well as any other officer or man there, but he knew more of the enemy's movements than did any other officer, old or young. He had "a special aptitude for war," says one general. "We used to send him to find out what new move the Russians were making."

Shortly after his adventure in the caves, Gordon had another narrow escape. A bullet fired at him from one of the Russian rifle-pits, 180 yards away, passed within an inch of his head. "It passed an inch above my nut into a bank I was passing," wrote Gordon, who had not forgotten his school-boy slang. But the only other remark he makes about his escape in his letter home is, "They (the Russians) are very good marksmen; their bullet is large and pointed."

Three months later, one of his brothers wrote home—"Charlie has had a miraculous escape. The day before yesterday he saw the smoke from an embrasure on his left and heard a shell coming, but did not see it. It struck the ground five yards in front of him, and burst, not touching him. If it had not burst, it would have taken his head off."

The shell struck the ground five yards in front of him

The soldiers at Sebastopol were not long in learning that amongst their officers there was one slight, wiry young lieutenant of sappers, with curly hair and keen blue eyes, who was like the man in the fairy tale, and did not know how to shiver and shake.

One day as Gordon was going the round of the trenches he heard a corporal and a sapper having hot words. He stopped and asked what the quarrel was about, and was told that the men were putting fresh gabions (baskets full of earth behind which they sheltered from the fire of the enemy's guns) in the battery. The corporal had ordered the sapper to stand up on a parapet where the fire from the guns would hail upon him, while he himself, in safety down below, handed the baskets up to him. In one moment Gordon had jumped up on to the parapet, and ordered the corporal to stand beside him while the sapper handed up baskets to them. The Russian bullets pattered around them as they worked, but they finished their work in safety. When it was done, Gordon turned to the corporal and said: "Never order a man to do anything that you are afraid to do yourself."

On 6th June there was a great duel between the guns of the Russians and those of their besiegers. A stone from a round shot struck Gordon, and stunned him for some time, and he was reported "Wounded" by the surgeon, greatly to his disgust. All day and all night, and until four o'clock next day, the firing went on. At four o'clock on the second day the English and their allies began to fire from new batteries. A thousand guns kept up a steady, terrible fire of shells, and, protected by the fire, the French dashed forward and seized one of the Russians' most important positions. Attacking and being driven back, attacking again and gaining some ground, once more attacking and losing what they had gained, leaving men lying dead and dying where the fight had been fiercest, so the weary days and nights dragged past.

"Charlie is all right," his brother wrote home, "and has escaped amidst a terrific shower of grape and shells of every description.... He is now fast asleep in his tent, having been in the trenches from two o'clock yesterday morning during the cannonade until seven last night, and again from 12-30 this morning until noon."

Both sides agreed to stop fighting for a few days after this, in order to bury the dead.

The whole ground before Sebastopol was, Gordon wrote, "one great graveyard of men, freshly made mounds of dark earth covering English, French, and Russians."

From this time until September the war dragged on. It was a dull and dreary time, and as September drew near Gordon thought of happy days in England, with the scent of autumn leaves, and the whir of a covey of birds rising from the stubble, and he longed for partridge-shooting. But they shot men, not birds, in the Crimea. "The Russians are brave," he wrote, "certainly inferior to none; their work is stupendous, their shell practice is beautiful." Gordon was never one to grudge praise to his enemies.

Every day men died of disease, or were killed or wounded. On 31st August 1855, Gordon wrote that "Captain Wolseley (90th Regiment), an assistant engineer, has been wounded by a stone." In spite of stones and shells, Captain Wolseley fought many brave fights, and years afterwards became Lord Wolseley, Commander-in-Chief of the British Army, a gallant soldier and a brilliant leader of men.

On 8th September one of the chief holds of the Russians was stormed by the French, who took it after a fierce fight and hoisted on it their flag. This was the signal for the English to attack the great fort of the Redan. With a rush they got to the ditch between them and the fortress, put up their ladders, and entered it. For half-an-hour they held it nobly. Then enormous numbers of fresh Russian troops came to the attack, and our men were driven out with terrible loss. At the same time, at another point, the French were driven back. Nothing was left for the allied troops but to wait till morning. It was decided that when morning came the Highland soldiers must storm and take the Redan. But this the Russians gave them no chance to do.

While Gordon was on duty in the trenches that night he heard a terrific explosion.

"At four next morning," he writes, "I saw a splendid sight. The whole of Sebastopol was in flames, and every now and then great explosions took place, while the rising sun shining on the place had a most beautiful effect. The Russians were leaving the town by the bridge; all the three-deckers were sunk, the steamers alone remaining. Tons and tons of powder must have been blown up. About eight o'clock I got an order to commence a plan of the works, for which purpose I went to the Redan, where a dreadful sight was presented. The dead were buried in the ditch—the Russians with the English—Mr. Wright" (an English chaplain), "reading the burial service over them."

The fires went on all day, and there were still some prowling Russians in the town, so that it was not safe to enter it.

When the allied forces did go in, they found many dreadful sights. For a whole day and night 3000 wounded men had been untended, and a fourth of them were dead. The town was strewn with shot and shell; buildings were wrecked, or burned down.

"As to plunder," wrote Gordon, "there is nothing but rubbish and fleas, the Russians having carried off everything else."

For some time after the fall of Sebastopol, Gordon and his men were kept busy clearing roads, burning rubbish, counting captured guns, and trying to make the town less unhealthy.

He then went with the troops that attacked Kinburn, a town many miles from Sebastopol, but also on the shores of the Black Sea. When it was taken, he returned to Sebastopol.

For four months he was there, destroying forts, quays, storehouses, barracks, and dockyards; sometimes being fired on by the Russians from across the harbour; never idle, always putting his whole soul into all that he did.

His work was finished in February 1856, and in March peace was declared between Russia and Britain.

The name of Lieutenant Gordon was included by his general in a list of officers who had done gallant service in the war.

By the French Government he was decorated with the Legion of Honour, a reward not often given to so young a man.

A little more than a year of hard training in war had turned Charlie Gordon the boy into Gordon the soldier.

In May 1856 Gordon was sent to Bessarabia, to help to arrange new frontiers for Russia, Turkey, and Roumania. In 1857 he was sent to do the same work in Armenia.

The end of 1858 saw him on his way home to England, a seasoned soldier, and a few months later he was made a captain.

CHAPTER III
"CHINESE GORDON"

For a year after his return from Armenia Gordon was at Chatham, as Field-Work Instructor and Adjutant, teaching the future officers of Engineers what he himself had learned in the trenches.

While he was there, a war that had been going on for some years between Britain and China grew very serious.

Gordon volunteered for service, but when he reached China, in September 1860, the war was nearly at an end. "I am rather late for the amusement, which won't vex mother," he wrote. He found, however, that a number of Englishmen, some of them friends of his, were being kept as prisoners in Pekin by the Chinese. The English and their allies at once marched to Pekin, and demanded that the prisoners should be given up.

The Chinese, scared at the sight of the armies and their big guns, opened the gates. But in the case of many of the prisoners, help had come too late. The Chinese had treated them most brutally, and many had died under torture.

Nothing was left for the allied armies to do but to punish the Chinese for their cruelty, and especially to punish the Emperor for having allowed such vile things to go on in his own great city.

The Emperor lived in a palace so gorgeous and so beautiful that it might have come out of the Arabian Nights. This palace the English general gave orders to his soldiers to pillage and to destroy. Four millions of money could not have replaced what was destroyed then. The soldiers grew reckless as they went on, and wild for plunder. Quantities of gold ornaments were burned for brass. The throne room, lined with ebony, was smashed up and burned. Carved ivory and coral screens, magnificent china, gorgeous silks, huge mirrors, and many priceless things were burned or destroyed, as a gardener burns up heaps of dead leaves and garden rubbish.

Treasures of every kind, and thousands and thousands of pounds' worth of exquisite jewels were looted by common soldiers. Often the men had no idea of the value of the things they had taken. One of them sold a string of pearls for 16s. to an officer, who sold it next day for £500. From one of the plunderers Gordon bought the Royal Throne, a gorgeous seat, supported by the Imperial Dragon's claws, and with cushions of Imperial yellow silk. You may see it if you go some day to the headquarters of the

Royal Engineers at Chatham, and you will be told that it was given to his corps by General Gordon.

After the sack of the Summer Palace Gordon had a very busy time, providing quarters for the English troops, helping to distribute the money collected for the Chinese who had suffered from the war, and doing surveying and exploring work. On horseback he and a comrade explored many places which no European had visited before, and many were their adventures.

But it was in work greater than this that "Chinese Gordon" was to win his title. While Gordon was a little boy of ten, a Chinese village schoolmaster, Hung-Tsue-Schuen, who came of a low half-gipsy race, had told the people of China that God had spoken to him, and told him that he was to overthrow the Emperor and all those who governed China, and to become the ruler and protector of the Chinese people.

Soon he had many followers, who not only obeyed him as their king, but who prayed to him as their god. He called himself a "Wang," or king, and his followers called him their "Heavenly King." He made rulers of some thousands of his followers—most of them his own relations—and they also were named Wangs, or kings. They also had their own special names, "The Yellow Tiger," "The One-Eyed Dog," and "Cock-Eye" were amongst these. Twenty thousand of his own clansmen, many of them simple country people, who believed all that he told them, joined him. There also joined him fierce pirates from the coast, robbers from the hills, murderous members of secret societies, and almost every man in China who had, or fancied he had, some wrong to be put right.

His army rapidly grew into hundreds of thousands.

When this host of savage-looking men, with their long lank hair, their gaudy clothes and many-coloured banners, their cutlasses and long knives, marched through the land, plundering, burning, and murdering, the hard-working, harmless little Chinamen, with their smooth faces and neat pigtails, fled before them in terror.

The Tae-Pings, as they came to be called, robbed them, slew them, burned their houses and their rice fields, and took their little children away from them. They flayed people alive; they pounded them to death. Ruin and death were left behind them as they marched on. Those who escaped were left to starvation. In some places so terrible was the hunger of the poor people that they became cannibals, for lack of any other food.

In one city which they destroyed, out of 20,000 people not 100 escaped.

"We killed them all to the infant in arms; we left not a root to sprout from; and the bodies of the slain we cast into the Yangtse,"—so boasted the rebels.

A march of nearly 700 miles brought this great, murdering, plundering army to Nanking, a city which the Wangs took, and made their capital. The frightened peasants were driven before them down to the coast, and took refuge in the towns there. Many of them had crowded into the port of Shanghai, and round Shanghai came the robber army. They wanted more money, more arms, and more ammunition, and they knew they could find plenty of supplies there. So likely did it seem that they would take the port, that the Chinese Government asked England and France to help to drive them away.

In May 1862 Gordon was one of the English officers who helped to do this. For thirty miles round Shanghai, the rebels, who were the fiercest of fighters, were driven back. In his official despatch Gordon's general wrote of him:—"Captain Gordon was of the greatest use to me." But he also said that Gordon often made him very anxious because of the daring way in which he would go dangerously near the enemy's lines to gain information. Once when he was out in a boat with the general, reconnoitring a town they meant to attack, Gordon begged to be put ashore so that he might see better what defences the enemy had.

To the general's horror, Gordon went nearer and nearer the town, by rushes from one shelter to another. At length he sheltered behind a little pagoda, and stood there quietly sketching and making notes. From the walls the rebels kept on firing at him, and a party of them came stealing round to cut him off, and kill him before he could run back to the boat. The general shouted himself hoarse, but Gordon calmly finished his sketch, and got back to the boat just in time.

The Tae-Pings used to drag along with them many little boys whose fathers and mothers they had killed, and whom they meant to bring up as rebels. After the fights between the English troops and the Tae-Pings, swarms of those little homeless creatures were always found.

Gordon writes: "I saved one small creature who had fallen into the ditch in trying to escape, for which he rewarded me by destroying my coat with his muddy paws in clinging to me."

In December 1862 Gordon, for his good service in China, was raised to the rank of major.

Very soon afterwards the Chinese Government asked the English Government to give them an English officer to lead the Chinese army that was to fight with, and to conquer, the Tae-Ping rebels.

Already the Chinese soldiers had been commanded by men who spoke English. One of these, an American adventurer, named Burgevine, was ready to dare anything for power and money.

To his leadership flocked scoundrels of every nation, hoping to enrich themselves by plundering the rebels.

Before long, Governor Li Hung Chang found that Burgevine was not to be trusted, and the command was taken from him.

It was then that the Chinese Government asked England to give them a leader for their untrained army of Chinese and of adventurers gathered from all lands. This collection of rag, tag, and bobtail had been named, to encourage it, and before it had done anything to deserve the name, the "Chun Chen Chün," or the Ever-Victorious Army.

But "The Almost Always Beaten Army" would have been a much truer name for it, and the victorious Tae-Pings scornfully laughed at it.

The English general in China had no doubt who was the best man for the post.

He named Major Charles Gordon, and on 25th March 1863 Gordon took command, and was given the title of Mandarin by the Chinese.

He knew that the idea of serving under any other monarch than his own Queen would be a sorrow to his father. He wrote home begging his father and mother not to be vexed, and telling them how deeply he had thought before he accepted the command.

By taking the command, he said, he believed he could help to put an end to the sufferings of the poor people of China. Were he not to have taken it, he feared that the rebels might go on for years spreading misery over the land. "I keep your likeness before me," wrote this young Major who had been trusted with so great a thing to do, to the mother whom he loved so much. "I can assure you and my father I will not be rash.... I really do think I am doing a good service in putting down this rebellion."

"I hope you do not think that I have got a magnificent army," he wrote to a soldier friend. "You never did see such a rabble as it was; and although I think I have improved it, it is still sadly wanting. Now, both men and officers, although ragged and perhaps slightly disreputable, are in capital order and well disposed."

Before his arrival, the soldiers had had no regular pay. They were allowed to "loot," or plunder, the towns they took, and for each town taken they were paid so much.

At once Gordon began to get his ragamuffin army into shape.

He arranged that the soldiers were to get their pay regularly, but were to have no extra pay for the places which they took. Any man caught plundering a town that was taken was to be shot. He replaced the adventurers of all nations, many of them drunken rogues, who were the army's officers, by English officers lent by the British Government. He drilled his men well. He practised them in attacking fortified places, and he formed a little fleet of small steamers and Chinese gunboats. The chief of these was the *Hyson*, a little paddle steamer that could move over the bed of a creek on its wheels when the water was too shallow to float it.

The army, too, was given a uniform, at which not only the rebels but the Chinese themselves at first mocked, calling the soldiers who wore it "Sham Foreign Devils."

But soon so well had Gordon's army earned its name of "The Ever-Victorious Army," that the mere sight of the uniform they wore frightened the rebels.

In one month Gordon's army was an army and not a rabble, and the very first battles that it fought were victories.

With 3000 men he attacked a garrison of 10,000 at Taitsan, and after a desperate fight the rebels were driven out.

From Taitsan the victorious army went on to Quinsan, a large fortified city, connected by a causeway with Soochow, the capital of the province.

All round Quinsan the country was cut up in every direction with creeks and canals. But Gordon knew every creek and canal in that flat land. He knew more now than any other man, native or foreigner, where there were swamps, where there were bridges, which canals were choked with weeds, and which were easily sailed up. He made up his mind that the rebels in Quinsan must be cut off from those in Soochow.

At dawn, one May morning, eighty boats, with their large white sails spread out like the wings of big sea-birds, and with many-coloured flags flying from their rigging, were seen by the rebel garrison at Quinsan sailing up the canal towards the city. In the middle of this fleet the plucky little *Hyson*, with Gordon on board, came paddling along.

By noon they reached a barrier of stakes placed across the creek. These they pulled up, sailed to the shore, and landed their troops close to the rebel stockades. For a minute the Tae-Pings stood and stared, uncertain what to do, and then, in terror, ran before Gordon's army.

There had been many boats in the creek, but the rebels had sprung out of them and a left them to drift about with their sails up, so that it was no easy work for the *Hyson* to thread her way amongst them. Still the little boat steamed slowly and steadily on towards Soochow. Along the banks of the canal the rebels, in clusters, were marching towards safety. On them the *Hyson* opened fire, puffing and steaming after them, and battering them with shells and bullets.

Like an angry little sheep-dog driving a mob of sheep, it drove the rebels onwards. Many lay dead on the banks, or fell into the water and were drowned. One hundred and fifty of them were taken as prisoners on board the *Hyson*.

When they were less than a mile from Soochow, as night was beginning to fall, Gordon decided to turn back and rejoin the rest of his forces. Some of the rebels, thinking that the *Hyson* was gone for good, had got into their boats again, and were gaily sailing up the creek when they saw the steamer's red and green lights, and heard her whistle.

The mere glare of the lights and hoot of the whistle seemed to throw them into a panic. In the darkness the flying mobs of men along the canal banks met other rebels coming to reinforce them, and in the wild confusion that followed the guns of the *Hyson* mowed them down. About 10.30 P.M. the crew of the *Hyson* heard tremendous yells and cheers coming from a village near Quinsan, where the rebels had made a stand. Gordon's gunboats were firing into the stone fort, and from it there came a rattle and a sparkle of musketry like fireworks, and wild yells and shouts from the rebels. The gunboats were about to give in and run away when the little *Hyson* came hooting out of the darkness. Gordon's army welcomed him with deafening cheers, and the rebels threw down their arms and fled. The *Hyson* steamed on up the creek towards Quinsan, and in the darkness Gordon saw a huge crowd of men near a high bridge. It was too dark to see clearly, but the *Hyson* blew her whistle. At once from the huddled mass of rebels came yells of fear. It was the garrison of Quinsan, some seven or eight thousand, trying to escape to Soochow. In terror they fled in every direction—8000 men fleeing before thirty. The *Hyson* fired as seldom as she could, but even then, that day the rebels must have lost from three to four thousand men, killed, drowned, and prisoners. All their arms also, they lost, and a great number of boats.

Next morning at dawn, Gordon and his army took possession of Quinsan. They had fought almost from daybreak until daybreak. "The rebels certainly never got such a licking before," wrote Gordon.

The Ever-Victorious Army was delighted with itself, and very proud of its leader. But they were less well-pleased with Gordon when they found that instead of going on to a town where they could sell the things they had managed to loot, they were to stay at Quinsan.

They were so angry that they drew up a proclamation saying that unless they were allowed to go to a town they liked better, they would blow their officers to pieces with the big guns. Gordon felt sure that the non-commissioned officers were at the bottom of the mischief. He made them parade before him, and told them that if they did not at once tell him the name of the man who had written the proclamation, he would have one out of every five of them shot. At this they all groaned, to show what a monster they thought Gordon. One corporal groaned louder than all the rest, and Gordon turned on him, his eyes blazing. So sure was Gordon that this was their leader that, with his own hands, he dragged him from the ranks.

With his own hands, he dragged him from the ranks

"Shoot this fellow!" he said to two of his bodyguard. The soldiers fired, and the corporal fell dead.

The other non-commissioned officers he sent into imprisonment for one hour.

"If at the end of that time," said he, "the men do not fall in at their officers' commands, and if I am not given the name of the writer of that proclamation, every fifth man of you shall be shot."

At the end of the hour the men fell in, and the name of the writer of the proclamation was given to Gordon. The man had already been punished. It was the corporal who had groaned so loud an hour before.

This was not the only case that Gordon had in his own army. More than once his officers were rebellious and troublesome. General Ching, a Chinese general, was jealous of him. Ching one day made his men fire on 150 of Gordon's soldiers, and treated it as a joke when Gordon was angry. At the beginning of the campaign Gordon had promised his men that they should have their pay regularly instead of plundering the places they took. His own pay, and more, had gone to do this and to help the poor. And now Li Hung Chang, the Governor, said he could not pay the men; and no one but Gordon seemed to mind when Ching broke his promise to prisoners who had been promised safety, and slew them brutally.

Disgusted with this want of honour and truth in the men with whom he had to work, Gordon made up his mind to throw up his command.

Just then, however, Burgevine, the adventurer, who had once led the Emperor's army, again became very powerful. He gathered together a number of men as reckless as himself, and joined the rebels. The rebels made him a Wang, or King, and he offered so much money to those who would serve under him that crowds of Gordon's grumbling soldiers deserted and joined Burgevine.

Burgevine and his followers were a grand reinforcement for the rebel army, and things began to look serious.

Gordon could not bear that the rebels should be allowed unchecked to swarm over China and plunder and slay innocent people. Instead of resigning he once more led the Ever-Victorious Army, and led it to victory.

Soochow, "The City of Pagodas," was besieged. There were twice as many soldiers in the town as there were besiegers, and amongst them were Burgevine and his men. In front of the city Gordon placed his guns, and after a short bombardment that did much damage to the walls, he ordered his troops to advance. A terrific fire from the enemy drove them back. Again Gordon's guns bombarded the city, and were pushed forward as far as possible. Then again the besiegers rushed in, but found that the creek round the city was too wide for the bridge they carried with them. But the officers plunged fearlessly into the water and dashed across. Their men followed them, the Tae-Pings fled, and stockade after stockade was taken. Gordon himself, with a mere handful of men, took three stockades and a stone fort.

In this siege, as in many other fights, Gordon had himself to lead his army. If an officer shrank back before the savage enemy, Gordon would take him gently by the arm and lead him into the thickest of the battle. He himself went unarmed, and would lead his troops onwards with the little cane he nearly always carried. Where the fire was hottest, there Gordon was always to be found, caring no more for the bullets that pattered round him than if they were hailstones. The Chinese soldiers came to look on the little cane as a magic wand. Gordon's "magic wand of victory," they called it.

During the siege he found men in his own army selling information to the rebels. One young officer, more out of carelessness, it seemed, than from any bad wish, had written a letter giving information to the enemy.

"I shall pass over your fault this time," said Gordon, "if you show your loyalty by leading the next forlorn hope."

Gordon forgot this condition, but the young officer did not. He led the next assault, was shot in the mouth, and fell back and died in the arms of Gordon, who was by his side.

A very wonderful old bridge, one of fifty-three arches, was destroyed during the siege of Soochow, greatly to Gordon's regret.

One evening he was sitting smoking a cigar on one of the damaged parapets of the bridge when two shots, accidentally fired by his own men, struck the stone on which he sat. At the second shot he got down, entered his boat, and started to row across the creek in order to find out by whom the shots had been fired. He was scarcely clear of the bridge than the part on which he had been seated fell crashing into the water, nearly smashing his boat.

The Chinese were more sure than ever that it must be magic that kept their general alive. Even when in a fierce fight he was severely wounded below the knee, they believed that his magic wand had saved his life.

From Soochow and the rebels he succeeded in rescuing Burgevine and his miserable followers, even although he knew that Burgevine was ready for any deed of treachery towards him at any minute.

One rebel stronghold after another fell before Gordon and his army, but many and fierce were the fights that were fought before Soochow was taken.

The Wangs gave in at last. They agreed to surrender if Gordon promised to spare the lives of the leading Wangs—six in all—to treat all the other rebels mercifully, and not to sack the city. To all these conditions Gordon, Li Hung Chang, and General Ching gladly agreed, and that night one of the gates was thrown open, and the Ever-Victorious Army took possession of Soochow.

As a reward for their brave service, and to make up to them for the loot they were not to have, Gordon asked Li Hung Chang to give his troops two months' pay. Li refused, but presently gave them pay for one month, and Gordon marched his grumbling soldiers back to Quinsan, unable to trust them in a city where so much rich plunder was to be had.

As Gordon left the city the Wangs, wearing no arms, and laughing and talking, rode past him on their way to a banquet with Li Hung Chang.

He never saw them alive again.

He had some time to wait for the steamer that was to take him to Quinsan, so, having seen his army marching safely off, he rode round the walls of the city. In front of Li Hung Chang's quarters he saw a great crowd, but so sure did he feel that Li would not break his solemn promises that he did not feel uneasy. A little later a large number of General Ching's men entered the city, yelling loudly, and firing off their guns. This was so unlike the peaceful way that Gordon and Ching had promised they should behave, that Gordon went and spoke to their officers.

"This will never do," he said. "There are still many rebels in the city, and if our men get excited the rebels will get excited too, and there will be fearful rioting."

Just then General Ching appeared. He had fancied Gordon safely steaming across the lake, and when he saw him he turned pale.

In answer to Gordon's questions as to the meaning of the disturbance, he gave some silly answer, which it was easy to see was untrue. Gordon at once rode to the house of Nar Wang, the chief of the Wangs and the bravest of them, to find out for himself what was wrong. On his way he met crowds of excited rebels, and a large band of Ching's soldiers laden with plunder. Nar Wang's house, he found, had been emptied of everything by the thieving soldiers. An uncle of Nar Wang begged Gordon to help him to take the women of Nar Wang's house to his own home, where they would be in safety. Unarmed as he was, Gordon did so, but when they got to the house of Nar Wang's uncle they found the courtyard filled with thousands of rebel soldiers. The doors and gates were shut at once, and Gordon was a prisoner. During the night more and more rebels came to the house. They all said that Li Hung Chang and Gordon had laid a trap for the Wangs and had taken them prisoners, but none knew exactly what had happened to them. It was well for Gordon that they did not. Probably they would have tortured him in one of the many hideous ways the Chinese knew so well, and then put him to death. At length Gordon persuaded his captors to allow him to send a messenger to summon his own bodyguard, and also an order to some of his other soldiers to seize Li

Hung Chang, and not to let him go until the Wangs had safely returned to their own homes.

On the way the messenger met some of Ching's soldiers, who wounded him and tore up Gordon's message. The rebels then allowed Gordon to be his own messenger; but on the way he met more of Ching's men, who seized him, because, they said, he was in company with rebels, and kept him prisoner for several hours.

When at last he got away and reached his own men, he sent a body of them to protect the house of Nar Wang's uncle. General Ching arrived just then. Gordon, furious with him for the looting and bad behaviour of his men, fell on him in a perfect storm of rage, and Ching hurried off to the city.

He sent an English officer to explain to Gordon what had happened, but this officer said he did not know whether the Wangs were alive or dead. He said, however, that Nar Wang's son was in his boat, and that he would be able to tell him.

"My father has been killed," said the boy. "He lies dead on the other side of the creek."

Gordon crossed the creek in a boat, and on the banks lay the dead bodies of the Wangs, headless, and frightfully gashed. Li Hung Chang and General Ching had broken their promise, and Gordon's. The guests of the banquet of Li Hung Chang had been cruelly murdered.

Many were the excuses that the Chinese Governor had to offer; many were the reasons that he gave for breaking faith so shamefully.

But to none of his excuses or reasons would Gordon listen. It is said that, in furious anger, he sought Li Hung Chang, revolver in hand, that he might shoot him like a dog. But Li wisely hid himself, and Gordon sought him in vain. He wrote to Li, telling him he must give up his post as Governor, or Gordon and his army would attack all the places the Chinese held, retake them, and hand them back to the rebels. His anger and his shame were equally great.

Li Hung Chang did the wisest thing that then could be done. He sent for Halliday Macartney, a wise and brave English officer, and a friend of Gordon's, and asked him to go to Gordon and try and make peace between them. Macartney at once got a native boat with several rowers, and started for Quinsan. It was the middle of the night when he arrived, and Gordon was in bed. Very soon, however, he sent Macartney a message, asking him to come and see him in his room. Macartney went upstairs and found

Gordon sitting on his bedstead in a badly lighted room. When Gordon saw him, he stooped down, drew something from under his bed, and held it up.

"Do you see that? Do you see that?" he asked.

Macartney stared in horror, scarcely able, in the dim light, to see what it was.

"It is the head of Nar Wang, foully murdered!" said Gordon, and sobbed most bitterly.

Halliday Macartney found it impossible then to get Gordon to forgive Li for his treachery. For two months Gordon remained in quarters, while inquiries, made at his demand, were being made about the death of the Wangs.

During this time the Chinese Government gave Gordon a medal that only the bravest soldiers ever received, to show how highly they valued his services as general. The Emperor also sent him a gift of 10,000 taels (then about £3000 of our money) and many other costly gifts. When the treasure-bearers appeared in Gordon's quarters, bearing bowls full of gold on their heads, as if they had walked straight out of the Arabian nights, Gordon, believing the Emperor meant to bribe him to say no more about the murder of the Wangs, was in a white-heat of fury. With his "magic wand" he fell on the treasure-bearers, and flogged the amazed and terrified men out of his sight.

Although the Government gave Gordon a medal for the way in which he had fought, it was Li Hung Chang who took all the credit for the taking of Soochow.

He published a report telling how the army under him had taken it. But while Gordon was under a daily fire of bullets, and daily ran a hundred risks of losing his life, the wily Li, who sounded so brave on paper, was safely sitting in Shanghai, miles away from the besieged city.

Gordon had much cause for anger. There seemed every reason why he should not forgive Li, and why he should leave China and its people to the mercy of the rebels.

But Gordon had learned what it means to say "Forgive us our trespasses." And not only that, but he had taken the sorrows of the unhappy people of China into his heart. Whatever their rulers might do, he felt he could not desert them. He must free them from the cruelties of their oppressors, the Tae-Pings, before he went home to his own land.

In February 1864 Gordon again took command. From then until 11th May he was kept constantly fighting, and steadily winning power for the Emperor of China.

On 10th May Gordon wrote to his mother: "I shall leave China as poor as I entered it, but with the knowledge that through my weak instrumentality upwards of eighty to one hundred thousand lives have been spared. I want no further satisfaction than this."

On 11th May Gordon took Chanchufu, the last great rebel stronghold, and the rebellion was at an end. "The Heavenly King" killed his wives and himself in his palace at Nankin, and the other rebel chiefs were beheaded.

Before Gordon gave up his command, the Chinese Government again offered him a large sum of money, but again he refused it. But he could not well refuse the honour of being made a Ti-Tu, or Field-Marshal, in the Chinese Army, nor the almost greater honour of being given the Yellow Jacket. To us the giving of a yellow jacket sounds a foolish thing, but to a Chinaman the Yellow Jacket, and peacock's feathers that go with it, are an even greater honour than to an Englishman is that plain little cross that is called "The Victoria Cross," and which is given for valour. Gordon accepted the yellow jacket, as well as six magnificent mandarin dresses, such as were worn by a Ti-Tu. "Some of the buttons on the mandarin hats are worth £30 or £40," he wrote. A heavy gold medal was struck in his honour and given to him by the Empress Regent. It was one of the few belongings he had for which Gordon really cared a great deal, and presently you will hear how he gave even that up for the sake of other people.

The Chinese Government told the British Government that Gordon would receive no rewards from the Chinese for the great things he had done for their country, and asked that his own Queen Victoria would give him some reward that he would accept. This was done, and Major Gordon was made a Lieutenant-Colonel and a Companion of the Bath.

Not only in China was he a hero, but in England also. Gordon had saved China from an army of conquering robbers, "first"—it was written in the *Times*—"by the power of his arms, and afterwards, still more rapidly, by the terror of his name."

Li Hung Chang was ready to do anything that the hero wished, and so, before he said good-bye to his army, Gordon saw that his officers and men were handsomely rewarded.

It was not wonderful that his army had learned to love him, for even the rebels who feared his name loved him too. They knew that he was always true and brave, honourable and merciful.

Of him one of the rebels wrote: "Often have I seen the deadly musket struck from the hand of a dastardly Englishman (tempted by love of loot to join our ranks) when he attempted from his place of safety to kill Gordon, who ever rashly exposed himself. This has been the act of a chief—yea, of the Shield King himself."

All England was ready to give "Chinese Gordon" a magnificent welcome when he came home. Invitations from the greatest in the land were showered upon him.

But when, early in 1865, he returned, he refused to be made a hero of.

"I only did my duty," he said, and grew quite shy and ashamed when people praised and admired him. He would accept no invitations, and it was only a very few people who were lucky enough to hear him fight his battles over again. Sometimes in the evening as he sat in the fire-light, in his father's house at Southampton, he would tell his eager listeners the wonderful tale of his battles and adventures in the far-off land of pagodas.

And to them not the least wonderful part of what they listened to was this, that the hero who was known all over the world as "Chinese Gordon" was one who took no credit for any of the great things he had done, and who was still as simple and modest as a little child.

CHAPTER IV
THE "KERNEL"

Had you lived thirty-five or forty years ago at Gravesend, a dirty, smoky town on the Thames near London, you might have read chalked up on doors and on hoardings in boyish handwriting, these words—

"GOD BLESS THE KERNEL."

And had you asked any of the ragged little lads that you met, who was "The Kernel," their faces would have lit up at once, while they told you that their "Kernel" was the best and bravest soldier in the world, and that his name was Colonel Gordon.

For six years after he left China, Gordon was Commanding Royal Engineer at Gravesend, and these years, he said, were "the most peaceful and happy of any portion of his life."

His work there was done, as all his work throughout his life was done, with all his might.

When he first took command he was worried by the amount of time that was wasted as he rowed from one port which he had to inspect, to another, in a pair-oared boat. He put away the pair-oared boat and got a four-oared gig, and soon had the men who pulled it trained to row him in racing style. They might sometimes have waited for hours on the chance of Colonel Gordon wanting them, but the minute his trim little figure was seen marching smartly down to the jetty, there was a rush for the boat. Almost before he was seated, the oars would be dipped and the men's backs bent as if they meant to win a boat race.

"A little faster, boys! a little faster!" Gordon would constantly say, and when he jumped ashore and hurried off to his work, he would leave behind him four very breathless men, who were proud of being the crew of the very fastest boat pulled in those waters.

The engineers under him he also trained never to lose any time,—always to do a thing not only as thoroughly and as well as possible, but as quickly as possible.

He would land at a port, and run up the steep earthworks in front of it, while his followers, many of them big, heavy men, would come puffing and panting after him.

One of his friends writes of him, "He was a severe and unsparing taskmaster, and allowed no shirking. No other officer could have got half the work out of the men that he did. He used to keep them up to the mark by exclaiming, whenever he saw them flag: 'Another five minutes gone, and this not done yet, my men! We shall never have them again.'"

The old-fashioned house, with its big old garden, which was Gordon's home during those six years, saw many strange guests during that time.

"His house," says one writer, "was school, and hospital, and almshouse in turn—was more like the abode of a missionary than of a Colonel of Engineers."

In his working hours he worked his hardest to serve his Queen and country. In the hours in which he might have rested or amused himself, he worked equally hard. And this other work was to serve the poor, the sick, the lonely, and to give a helping hand to every one of those who needed help. The boys whose work was on the river or the sea, and the "mud-larks" of Gravesend, were his special care. Many a boy who had no work and no right home, he took from the streets, washed, clothed, fed, and took into his house to stay with him as his guest. When he had found work for those boys, either as sailors or in other ways, he would give them outfits and money, and start them in life. For the boys who were being sheltered by him, and for others from outside, he began evening classes. There he taught them, and read to them, and did all that he could to make them Christian gentlemen. His "Kings" he called them, perhaps remembering the many Kings or "Wangs" who ruled in the Tae-Ping army.

A map of the world, hanging over his mantelpiece, was stuck full of pins. Some one asked the meaning of this, and was told by Gordon that they marked and followed the course of his boys on their voyages. The pins were moved from point to point as the boys sailed onward. "I pray for each one of them day by day," he said.

Soon Gordon's class grew too big for his room to hold, and he then began to have a class at the Ragged Schools. The mud-larks of Gravesend needed no coaxing to go to "The Kernel's" class. Here was a teacher who did not only try to teach them to be good and manly, and straight and true, and *gentle* men, but who, when he taught them geography, could tell them the most splendid and exciting stories of countries beyond the seas, where he himself had fought in great battles. He never *preached* at them, or looked solemn and shocked, but made them laugh more than any one else ever did, and had the merriest twinkle in his kind, keen eyes, that were like the sea, and looked sometimes blue, sometimes grey.

He found out one day that what his "Kings" most longed to do was to go up to London to see the Zoo. No sooner did he know it than every plan was made for the little campaign. He himself could not leave his work, but he got some one else to take them, saw them safely off with their dinner in baskets, and welcomed them back in the evening to a great strawberry feast.

Three or four of the boys who stayed with him got scarlet fever, and far into the night he would sit with them, telling them stories, and soothing them until they stopped tossing about and fell asleep.

At first, when he came to Gravesend, he clothed two or three boys in the year. But it was not long before he gave away, each year, several hundreds of suits, and had to buy boys' boots by the gross.

All this came out of his pay. Gordon was always well-dressed, well-groomed, and looked like an officer and a gentleman, but upon himself he spent next to nothing.

His food was of the plainest, and sometimes of the scantiest. He would tell, with a twinkle in his eye, what a surprise it was to the boys who came to stay with him, expecting to be fed with all sorts of dainties, to find that salt beef, and just what other things were necessary, was what the Colonel had to eat.

Constantly his purse and pockets were empty, for scarcely ever did any one come to Gordon for help without getting it, and Gordon had no money save his pay as a colonel.

Often he had disappointments. There were people who were mean enough to deceive him, and people with no gratitude in their hearts.

One boy he found starving, in rags, and miserably ill. He fed him, clothed him, had him doctored and nursed, and, when he was well, sent him back to his parents in Norfolk. But neither boy nor parents ever sent him one line of thanks.

Another starving, ragged boy he took into his house. He fed, clothed, and taught him, and at last found him a good place on a ship, and sent him to sea. Three times did this little scamp run away from the ship, and turn up filthy, starving, and in rags. The third time Gordon found him in the evening lurking at the door, half dead with hunger and cold. The boy was much too dirty to be brought into the house with other boys, and Gordon looked at him for a minute in silence. He then led him to the stable, gave him a heap of clean straw in an empty stall to sleep on, and some bread and milk for supper. Early next morning Gordon appeared with soap, towels, a brush, a sponge, and a fresh suit of clothes. He poured a bucket of hot water into the horse trough, and himself gave him a thorough scrubbing.

Gordon appeared with soap, towels, a brush, a sponge, and a fresh suit of clothes

We do not know what afterwards became of the boy. It would be nice to think that he was the unknown man who came to the house of Sir Henry Gordon, when the news of General Gordon's death was heard, and wished to give £25 towards a memorial to him. "All my success and prosperity I owe to the Colonel," he said.

There were many boys—there are many men now—with good cause for saying from their hearts, "*God bless the Colonel.*"

A boy, who worked in a shop, stole some money from his master, who was very angry, and said he would have him put in prison. The boy's mother, in a terrible state of grief, came to Gordon and begged him to help her. Gordon went to the boy's master, and persuaded him to let the boy off. He then sent the little lad to school for twelve months, and afterwards found him a berth at sea. The boy has grown up into an honest, good man. "God bless the Colonel," he, too, can say.

Two afternoons a week Gordon went to the infirmary, to cheer up the sick people there. And in all parts of Gravesend he would find out old and bedridden men and women, sit with them, cheer them up with tales of his days in Russia and China, and make them feel less lonely and less sad. "He always had handy a bit o' baccy for the old men, and a screw o' tea for the old women," it was said.

One poor, sick old woman was told by the doctor that she must have some dainties and some wine, which she had no money to buy. But each day a good fairy brought them to her, and the good fairy was Colonel Gordon.

A sick man, who lay fretting in bed, feeling there was nothing to do, nothing to interest him, found each day a *Daily News* left at his door. Again the good fairy was Colonel Gordon.

A big, rough waterman, tossing about in bed with an aching, parched throat, and in a burning fever, also knew the good fairy. Night after night the Colonel sat by his bed, tending him as gently as the gentlest nurse, and placing cool grapes in his parched mouth.

In the Colonel's big, old-fashioned garden, with its trim borders of boxwood, one would find on summer days the old and the halt sunning themselves. Many nice flowers and vegetables were grown in the garden, but they did not belong to him. He allowed some of his poor people to plant and sow there what vegetables they chose, and then to make money for themselves by selling them.

Presents of fruit and flowers sent to him at once found their way to the hospital or to the workhouse. People saw that it was no use ever to give Gordon any presents, because they at once went to those who needed the things more than he did.

To the poor he gave pensions of so much a week—from 1s. to £1. Some of these pensions were still kept up and paid to the day of his death, thirteen years later.

He was always tender-hearted, always merciful, and he *always* forgave.

A soldier got tipsy, and stole five valuable patent locks. Gordon asked the manager of the works from which they had been taken what he meant to do.

"The carpenters were to blame for leaving the locks about, so I am going to let the soldier off," said the manager.

"Thank you, thank you," said Gordon, as eagerly as if he himself had been the thief. "That is what I should have done myself."

One day a woman called on him and told him a piteous story. He left the room to get her half-a-sovereign, and while he was gone she stole his overcoat, and hid it under her skirt. When he came back with the money, she thanked him again and again, and went away. As she walked along the street, the overcoat—a brown one—slipped down. A policeman noticed it, and asked her what it meant. The woman, too frightened to tell a lie, said she had stolen it from "the Kernel." Back to Gordon's house the policeman marched her. The coat was shown to Gordon, and the policeman asked him to charge the woman with the theft, and have her put in prison. But this Gordon refused to do. He was really far more distressed than was the thief herself. At last, his eyes twinkling, he turned to the woman.

"You wanted it, I suppose?" he asked.

"Yes," said the surprised woman.

"There, there, take her away and send her about her business," he said to the policeman, and the policeman could only obey.

The gold medal which the Empress of China had had made for him mysteriously disappeared, no one could tell how or where. Years afterwards, by accident, it was found that Gordon had had the inscription taken off it, and had sent it anonymously to Manchester, to help to buy food for the people who were starving there because of the Cotton Famine. It cost him so much to give it up that often, when he meant that others should give up something that was to cost them a very great deal, he would say, "You must give up your medal."

"In slums, hospitals, and workhouse, or knee-deep in the river at work upon the Thames defence," so he spent the six happiest years of his life.

In 1871, to the deep sorrow of all Gravesend, he was made British Commissioner to the European Commission of the Danube, where he had done good work fifteen years earlier.

To his "Kings" at the Ragged Schools he left a number of magnificent Chinese flags, trophies of his victories in China. They are still carried aloft every year at school treats, and the name of their giver is cheered until the echoes ring and voices grow hoarse.

To the people of Gravesend, and to people of all lands who hear the story of those six years, he left the memory of a man whose charity was perfect, whose mercy was without limit, and whose faith in the God he served was never-failing.

CHAPTER V
GORDON AND THE SLAVERS

Gordon went to his work on the Danube on 1st October 1871, and remained there until 1873.

On his return to England then, his short visit was a sad one. While he was home his mother became paralysed, and no longer knew the son she loved so much; and the death took place of his youngest brother, who had shared his pranks in the long-ago happy days at Woolwich.

In the same year the Khedive of Egypt asked Gordon to come, at a salary of £10,000 a year, to be Governor of the tribes on the Upper Nile.

Gordon accepted the post, but would not take more than £2000 a year. He wished, he said, "to show the Khedive and his people that gold and silver idols are not worshipped by all the world." He knew that the money was wrung from the poor people of Egypt and that some of it was the price of slaves, and he could not bear to enrich himself with money so gained.

The Soudan, or Country of the Blacks, which was now to be the scene of Gordon's work, is one of the dreariest parts of Africa.

In years not so long ago, the Egyptians had nothing to do with it. For between Egypt and the Black People's country lay hundreds of miles of sandy desert—desolate, lonely, without water. Behind its rocks the wild desert tribes could hide, to surprise and murder peaceful traders who tried to bring their camel caravans across the waste of sand. And when the desert was crossed and the Soudan reached, the country was not one to love or to long for.

A wretched, dry land is the Soudan, a land across which hot winds sweep, like blasts from a furnace, driving the sand before them. The Nile wanders through it, but in the Soudan there is none of the green and pleasant river country that we know, who know the Thames and the Tweed, the Hudson or St. Lawrence.

There is never a fresh leaf, never a blade of grass. The hills are bare slopes, the valleys strewn with sand and stones. Tufts of rough yellow grass and stunted grey bushes, a mass of thorns, grow here and there on the yellow sand. The mimosa trees, sapless and dry, are thick with thorns. The palms, called dom-palms, grow fruit like wood. The Sodom apples, that look like real fruit, are poisonous and horrible to the taste.

Tarantulas, scorpions, serpents, white ants, mosquitoes, and every kind of loathsome creature that flies and crawls is to be found there.

When men are toiling through that land, dust in their throats, sand in their eyes, and longing with all their hearts for the sight of something green, and the touch and taste of fresh, cool, sparkling water, sometimes they see a great wonder.

In front of them suddenly appears a lake or river, sparkling and shimmering. There is green grass at the water-side. White-winged birds float on it, and trees dip their leafy branches into its coolness. Sometimes great palaces and towers overlook it. Sometimes it seems a lonely spot, quiet and peaceful, and delicious for the weary wanderers to rest at.

English soldiers have often started off running with their empty water-bottles to fill them in that lake or river. Many, many travellers have hastened towards it when they knew that they must have water or die. But ever the mirage, as it is called, retreats before them. That water is like magic water that no human being can ever drink. The palaces and towers are like fairy palaces and towers into which no real person ever enters. The green leaves and white birds, the trees and the grass, are only a picture that the sun and the desert make to madden thirst-parched men.

"When Allah made the Soudan," say the Arabs, "he laughed."

European traders were amongst the first to open a way into the Soudan. The Egyptians knew that there was much fine ivory to be got there, but were too lazy to try to get it. The Europeans, many of them Englishmen, braved dangers and hardships, and made much money by the ivory they bought from the black people of the desert land. Soon they found there was something else for which they could get much higher prices than any that they could get for elephants' tusks. They called it "black ivory." By that they meant slaves.

At once they began to raid, to harry, and to kidnap the black races of the Soudan. They built forts and garrisoned them with Arabs, to whom no cruelty was too frightful, no wickedness too great. They burned down the villages of the blacks. They stole their flocks and herds. They burned or stole their crops. Their wives and little children they tore from them, chained them in gangs, and took them across the desert to sell for slaves. The men whom they could not take they slew.

So great and shameless became this trade, that at last Europe grew ashamed that any of her people should be guilty of it. There was an outcry made. The Europeans sold their stations to the Arabs, and quietly withdrew. The Arabs then agreed to pay a tax to the Egyptian Government, which saw no harm in stealing people and selling them as slaves, so long as some of the money thus gained went into the royal treasury.

And so the slave trade grew and grew, until, in 1874, out of every hundred people of the land about eighty-four were slaves. The Arabs trained some of the black boys they caught to be slave-hunters, and taught them so well that they grew up even more wicked and cruel than their masters.

Before long the slavers became so powerful and so rich that they no longer owned the Khedive as their king. Their king was Sebehr, the richest and worst of them all—a man who used to have chained lions as part of his escort, and who owned a great army of armed slaves. When the slavers refused to pay a tax any longer, and when they had cut in pieces the army the Khedive sent to quell them, the Khedive grew afraid.

He knew that England and the other European Powers were angry with him because he permitted slavery. And now that the slavers refused to obey him, he was between two fires.

So the Khedive and his ministers suddenly seemed to become very much shocked at the wicked traffic in slaves in the Soudan, and asked Colonel Gordon to come and help to stop it.

Early in February Gordon arrived in Cairo. He had been but a few days there when he wrote: "I think I can see the true motive now of the expedition, and believe it to be a sham to catch the attention of the English people." He felt he had been humbugged. Only in name was he Governor, for the Egyptian Government only owned three stations in that wide tract of country which he had been asked to come and govern.

But Gordon never turned his back upon those who wanted help. The land was full of misery. There were thousands of wretched people to fight for and to set free. Humbugged or not, he must do the work he had come to do, and on the 18th of February 1874 he started for the Soudan.

The Egyptian troops and Gordon's own staff were amazed when they found what sort of a man was the new Governor. They were used to the Egyptian officials who never did any work they were not paid for, who did not do it then if they could find any one else to do it for them, and whose hands were constantly held out asking for bribes.

Sebehr the slaver, when he went to Cairo, took with him £100,000 to bribe the Pashas. It was as if some notorious criminal should go to London with £100,000 gained by murders and thefts to bribe the British Government. But what would be outrageous in our country was a very usual thing in Egypt.

As Gordon and his troops (200 Egyptian soldiers) sailed up the Nile in their *dahabeah*, the boat was often blocked by the tangled water weeds. And always one of the first to spring into the water and help to pull the boat onwards was the new Governor. The old Nile crocodiles, even, must have been surprised; but they did him no harm, for they never touch any one who is moving.

They landed at Berber, and after a fortnight's march across the desert they reached the two or three thousand yellowish-white, flat-roofed, mud-walled houses that made Khartoum, the capital of the Soudan.

There eight busy days were spent. He issued proclamations; he held a review; he visited the hospitals and the schools. "The little blacks were glad to see me," he wrote; "I wish the flies would not dine on the corners of their eyes."

The grown-up people at Khartoum also seemed delighted to see "His Excellency General Colonel Gordon, the Governor-General of the Equator," as his title went. "They make a shrill noise when they see you, as a salutation; it is like a jingle of bells, very shrill, and somewhat musical," wrote Gordon.

From Khartoum he sailed up the Nile to Gondokoro, and enjoyed like a boy all the new sights he came across.

Hoary old crocodiles lay basking on the sand, their hungry mouths agape. Great hippopotamuses, "like huge islands," walked about in the shallows, and sometimes bellowed and fought all night. Troops of monkeys, "with very long tails stuck up straight like swords all over their backs," came down to drink. Herds of elephants and of fierce, coal-black buffaloes eyed the boat threateningly from the banks, while giraffes, looking like steeples, nibbled the tops of trees. At Khartoum the sight of flocks of English sparrows had gladdened Gordon's heart. Now he saw storks and geese preparing to go north for the summer, and many strange birds as well. He found out that some little white birds that roosted in the trees near where he camped were white egrets. Their feathers make the plumes of horse artillery officers, and trim many hats and bonnets, so Gordon did not tell his men of his discovery. "I do not want the poor things to be killed," he wrote.

Not only strange birds and beasts were to be seen on the way to Gondokoro. The wild black people came down to the banks to stare. Some had their faces smeared with ashes, others wore gourds for headdresses. Some wore neither gourds nor anything else. One chieftain's full dress was a string of beads. At first he was afraid to come near Gordon, but when he had been given a present of beads and other things he grew very friendly.

"He came up to me," says Gordon, "took up each hand, and gave a good soft lick to the backs of them; and then he held my face and made the motion of spitting in it."

This was a mark of great politeness and respect. A chief of this tribe once welcomed an English traveller by spitting into each of his hands, and then into his face. The traveller, in a rage, spat back as hard as ever he could, and the chief was overcome with joy at the traveller's friendliness.

Near Gondokoro, at St. Croix, Gordon came to the ruins of an Austrian missionary settlement. Only a few banana trees, planted by the missionaries, and some graves, marked where the Christian settlement had been. Out of twenty missionaries who had gone there during thirteen years, thirteen had died of fever, two of dysentery, and two, broken in health, had had to go home. And yet they had not been able to claim as a Christian even one of the blacks amongst whom they worked. No wonder that the Austrian Government lost heart and gave up the mission.

When Gordon reached Gondokoro he saw that it was absurd to pretend that the Khedive ruled any of the country outside its walls. No one dared go half a mile outside without being in danger of his life from the tribes whose wives and children and cattle the slavers had taken.

Gordon felt that to make friends with those people, to show them that he was sorry for them, and that he wished to help them, was the first thing to be done if he was to be in reality their Governor. And so, as he travelled on from point to point—back to Khartoum from Gondokoro, to Berber, to Fashoda, to Soubat—he made friends wherever he went. Quickly the black people came to love the man who punished or slew their enemies, who took them from the slavers, and gave them back their wives and children and cattle. He gave grain to some, set others to plant maize, fed the starving ones, and always paid them for each piece of work that they did for him.

Sometimes, even, he would buy from them the children that they were too poor to feed, and find good homes for them.

One man sold him his two boys of twelve and eight for a basket of dhoora (a kind of grain). He soon found that the blacks did not look on the sale of human beings in the same way that he did.

In the Soudan buying two children for a basketful of dhoora

In the Soudan buying two children for a basketful of dhoora

One man stole a cow, and when the owner found out the thief and came to claim his cow, it was too late. The cow had been eaten.

Next day Gordon passed the man's hut, and saw that one of his two children was gone.

"Where was the other?" he asked of the mother.

"Oh, it had been given to the man from whom the cow had been stolen," she replied with a happy smile.

"But," said Gordon, "are you not sorry?"

"Oh no! we would rather have the cow."

"But you have eaten the cow, and the pleasure is over," said Gordon.

"Oh, but, all the same, we would sooner have the cow!"

Two little boys came smiling up to Gordon one day, and pressed him to buy one of them for a little basketful of dhoora. Gordon bought one, and both boys were delighted.

"Do buy me for a little piece of cloth. I should like to be your slave," said one little fellow that Gordon rescued from a gang of slavers. It was this boy, Capsune, who years afterwards asked Gordon's sister if she was quite sure that Gordon Pasha still kept his blue eyes. "Do you think he can see all through me now?" he asked, and said, "I am quite sure Gordon Pasha could see quite well in the dark, because he has the light inside him."

Most of the slaves that the Arab slavers had in their gangs were little children. In one caravan that Gordon rescued there were ninety slaves, very few over sixteen, most of them little mites of boys and girls, perfect skeletons. They had been brought over 500 miles of desert, and the ninety were all that lived out of about four hundred.

When Gordon rescued them, they knew the gentle, tender Gordon, whose tenderness was like a mother's.

It was another Gordon that the slavers knew—a man terrible in his anger. Having taken from the ruffianly Arabs who had so cruelly treated the little children, their slaves, their stolen cattle, and their ivory, he would have them stripped and flogged, and driven naked into the desert.

For two months he was at Saubat River, a lonely and desolate country, the prey of slavers. It was so dull and dreary a place, that the Arab soldiers were sent there for a punishment, as the Russians are sent to Siberia.

But Gordon was too busy to be dull. He was always so full of thought for others, that he never had time to be sorry for himself.

"*I am sure it is the secret of true happiness to be content with what we actually have*," he wrote from Saubat.

From there, too, he wrote: "I took a poor old bag-of-bones into my camp a month ago, and have been feeding her up; but yesterday she was quietly taken off, and now knows all things. She had her tobacco up to the last."

Looking out of his camp he saw a poor woman, "a wisp of bones," feebly struggling up the road in wind and rain. He sent some dhoora to her by one of his men, and thought she had been taken safely to one of the huts. All through that wet and stormy night he heard a baby crying. At dawn he found the woman lying in a pool of mud, apparently dead, while men passed and repassed her, and took no notice. Her baby, not quite a year old, sat and wailed in some long grass near her. The woman was actually not dead, but she died a few days later. The baby boy was none the worse for his night out, and drank off a gourd of milk "like a man." Gordon gave him to a family to look after, paying for him daily with some maize.

Mosquitoes and other insects were a pest wherever he went, but at Saubat he had the extra pest of rats. They ran over his mosquito nets, ate his soap, his books, his boots, and his shaving-brush, and screamed and fought all night, until he invented a clever trap and stopped their thefts.

When Gordon returned to Gondokoro, he found nearly all his own staff ill with fever and ague. Out of ten only two were well,—one of these having newly recovered from a severe fever. Two were dead, and six seriously ill. Gordon himself was worn to a mere shadow, but he had to act as doctor and as sick-nurse. The weather was cold and wet, and the rain came into the tents. To his sister, Gordon wrote: "Imagine your brother paddling about a swamped tent without boots, attending to a sick man at night, with more than a chance of the tent coming down bodily." Of course he got chilled, and ill too, and at last gave an order that "all illness is to take place away from me."

Nor was it only sickness amongst his friends that he had to sadden him. He found that his Egyptian officials—some of them those he had most trusted—were leaguing with the slavers, taking bribes, helping to undo the good work he had already done, and trying to rouse his troops into mutiny. The troops themselves were a great trial. They were lazy, treacherous, chicken-hearted fellows, with no pluck. "I never had less confidence in any troops in my life," Gordon said, and he declared that three natives would put a whole company to flight. The native Soudanese were as brave as lions. A native has been known to kill himself because his wife called him a coward. The Arab soldiers when on sentry duty would all go to sleep at their posts, and think no harm of it.

The climate of the Soudan did not suit them, and they died like flies. Of one detachment of 250, half were dead in three months, 100 invalided, and only twenty-five fit for duty, and yet the Egyptian Government continued to send them instead of the black troops Gordon asked for.

From Gondokoro, Gordon moved to Rageef, and there built a station on healthier ground, higher up from the marshes. He sent to Gondokoro for ammunition for his mountain howitzer, and the commandant there thought it a good chance to pawn off on him some that was so damp as to be useless. With ten men and no ammunition, his Arab allies left him in a place where no Arab would have stayed without 100 well-armed men.

Gordon's German servant, and two little black boys that Gordon had bought, followed in a small boat to Rageef with Gordon's baggage.

The German came to Gordon with very grave face.

"I have had a great loss," said he. Gordon at once thought that one of the boys must have been drowned.

"What?" he anxiously asked.

"I saw a hippopotamus on the bank," said the man, "and fired at him with your big rifle; and I did not know it would kick so hard, and it kicked me over, and it fell into the water."

Said Gordon, "You are a born idiot of three years old! How dare you touch my rifle?"

But the rifle was gone, and he had to smile as the little black boys mimicked the German's fright when he dropped the rifle and laughed in scorn at him.

At Rageef, seeing he need expect no real help from the Egyptian Government, Gordon began to form an army of his own, making soldiers of the Soudanese,—the "Gippies," as our own soldiers now call them. And the Gippies are as brave and soldier-like a body of troops as is to be found. "We," they say, "are like the English; we are not afraid." He enlisted men who had been slaves, and men who had been slavers. A detachment of cannibals that he came across he also enlisted, drilled, and trained, and turned into first-rate soldiers.

The slavers grew afraid of Gordon Pasha, and of the army that he had made.

Where an Egyptian official would not have dared to go without a convoy of 100 soldiers, and where a single soldier would have been sure to have been waylaid and murdered, Gordon could now go in safety, alone and unarmed. He would walk along the river banks for miles and miles, only armed when he wished to shoot a hippopotamus.

Gordon's work was always much varied. Always, each bit of it was done with all his might.

He drilled savages, shot hippopotamuses, mended watches and musical boxes for black chiefs, patched his own clothes and made clothes for some of his men, invented rat-traps and machines for making rockets, tamed baby lions and baby hippopotamuses, cleaned guns, raided the camps of slavers, nursed the sick, and fed the hungry. And day and night he worked to rid the land of slavery; to teach the black people the meaning of justice, of mercy, and of honour.

His food all the time was of the plainest—no vegetables, only dry biscuits, bits of broiled meat, and macaroni boiled in sugar and water. Ants and beetles often nested in the stores, and made them horrid to the taste. "Oh, how I should like a good dinner!" he wrote to his sister.

In addition to all his other work, Gordon had the task of finding out for himself the exact geography of that part of the Nile of which he was Governor, and he had to do much exploring.

While doing this he one day marched 18 miles through jungle, in pouring rain. Another day, in the hottest season of that hot land, he marched 35 miles.

As he and his men sailed up the Nile they met with many dangers. There were rapids to pass, furious hippopotamuses to charge their boats, and on the banks were concealed enemies, throwing their assegais with deadly aim. And through all this he had only a pack of cowardly Arabs to depend on for everything.

A wizard belonging to one of the black tribes, sure that the white man and his soldiers could only have come for some evil purpose, stood on the top of a rock by the river, screaming curses at them and exciting his tribe.

"I don't think that's a healthy spot to deliver an address from," said Gordon, taking up a rifle and pointing it at the wizard, who at once ran away.

"We do not want your beads; we do not want your cloth; we only want you to go away," one tribe said to him. Gordon's heart was full of pity for them. It was for them that he was spending his life, had they only known it.

The never-ending work and worry tried him badly.

"Poor sheath, it is much worn," he wrote of himself from the dreary land of marsh and forest into which he had come while laying down a chain of posts between Gondokoro and the Lakes.

The dampness of the marshes was poison to white men, and earwigs, ants, mosquitoes, sandflies, beetles, scorpions, snakes, and every imaginable insect and reptile seemed to do their best to make things unpleasant for him.

The turf was full of prickly grass seeds; the long grass cut the fingers to the bone if people tried to pick it. The very fruit was bitter and poisonous. Rain sometimes fell in unexpected torrents, so heavy that he was flooded out of his tent.

When he was dead tired, body and soul, Gordon would sometimes build castles of what he would do when he got back to England. He would lie in bed till eleven, and always wear his best fur coat, and travel first class, and have oysters every day for lunch!

In 1876 there seemed a chance of his really building his castles.

He felt it was impossible to rid the land of slavery, with the Egyptian officials, who did not wish to have it stopped, working hard against him, and so, after three years of hard work, he threw up his post and went home.

No sooner was he gone than the Khedive realised how great a loss it would be to him and to his country if Gordon were not to return.

He begged him to come back, and he would make him Governor-General of the Soudan, and help him in every possible way to carry out the work he wished to do.

So Gordon returned, and in February 1877 he started for the Soudan, absolute ruler now of 1640 miles of desert, marsh, and forest.

"So there is an end of slavery," he wrote to his sister, "if God wills, for the whole secret of the matter is in that Government (the Soudan), and if the man who holds the Soudan is against it, it must cease." ... "I go up alone with an infinite Almighty God to direct and guide me, and am glad to so trust Him as to fear nothing, and, indeed, to feel sure of success."

From this time on, in every direction, the slavers were hunted and harried and driven out of the land, as one drives rats from a farmyard.

On every side he came on caravans packed with starving slaves, dying of hunger and thirst, and set them free. The desert was strewn not only with the bodies of camels, that the dry air had turned into mummies, but with the bones and whitened skulls of the slave-dealers' victims. Everywhere he had to look out for treachery and for lying, and be ready to pounce on slaves cunningly concealed by the kidnappers.

A hundred or more would sometimes be found being smuggled past, down the Nile, hidden under a boatload of wood.

Gordon, on a camel that he rode so quickly that it came to be called the Telegraph, seemed to fly across the silent desert like a magician. Daily, often all alone, he would ride 30 or 40 miles. In the three years during which he governed the Soudan he rode 8490 miles.

The black people knew that he was always willing to listen to their troubles, always ready to help them. In the first three days of his governorship he gave away over £1000 of his own money to the hungry poor.

Great chiefs, as well as poor people, came to see him and became his friends. If one of them sat too long, Gordon would rise and say in English: "Now, old bird, it is time for you to go," and the chief would go away, delighted with the Governor's affability and politeness. Those who begged, and continued to beg for things he could not grant, knew a different Governor.

"Never!" he would shout in an angry voice. "Do you understand? Have you finished?" and they would hurry off, frightened at his flashing eyes.

When fighting was necessary, he led his men as he had led his Chinese troops in past days. Like Nelson, he did not know the meaning of the word "fear."

News came to him that the son of Sebehr, king of the slavers, with 6000 men, was about to attack a poor, weak little garrison that they could have wiped out with the greatest ease. At once Gordon mounted his camel, and, alone and unarmed, sped off across the desert, covering 85 miles in a day and a half. On the way he rode into a swarm of flies that thickly covered him and his camel. Of his arrival at the little garrison he wrote to his sister: "I came on my people like a thunderbolt.... Imagine to yourself a single, dirty, red-faced man on a camel, ornamented with flies, arriving in the divan all of a sudden. They were paralysed, and could not believe their eyes."

Still more paralysed were the slavers when, at dawn next morning, there rode into their camp Gordon Pasha, radiant in the gorgeous "golden armour" the Khedive had given him. Fearlessly and scornfully Gordon condemned them, and ordered them at once to lay down their arms. They listened in silence and wonderment, and then weakly submitted to this great Pasha who knew no fear.

There rode into their camp Gordon Pasha (page 04)

There rode into their camp Gordon Pasha

When the slavers' power had been broken and their dens harried out—not without some heavy fighting—Gordon went on a mission from the Khedive to the King of Abyssinia, one of the cruellest and most savage of cruel kings. The Khedive wanted peace, but the Abyssinian King would not have it, and treated Gordon with the greatest insolence.

"Do you know that I could kill you?" he asked, glaring at Gordon like a tiger. Gordon answered that he was quite ready to die, and that in killing him the King would only confer a favour on him, opening a door he must not open for himself.

"Then my power has no terrors for you?" said the King.

"None whatever," replied Gordon, and the King, who was used to rule by terror, had no more to say.

This mission over, Gordon, utterly worn out, and broken in health, returned to Egypt, and resigned his post as Governor-General of the Soudan.

The slaves that he had set free used to try to kiss his feet and the hem of his garment. To this day there is a name known in Egypt and in the Soudan as that of a man who scorned money, who had no fear of any man, who did not even fear death, whose mercy was as perfect as his uprightness. And the name of that man is Gordon Pasha.

"Give us another Governor like Gordon Pasha," was the cry of the Soudanese when the Mahdi uprose to be a scourge to the Soudan.

CHAPTER VI KHARTOUM

Gordon left Egypt in December 1879, "not a day too soon," the doctor said, for he was ill, not only from hard work, but from overwork.

The burden he had carried on his shoulders through those years was the burden of the whole of the Soudan.

He was ordered several months of complete rest. But those days of rest were only castles that Gordon had built in his day-dreams, when burning days and bitter nights had made him long for ease.

Early in 1880 he became Secretary to Lord Ripon, Viceroy of India. He remained only a few months in India, and then went to China, in answer to an urgent message from his old friend, Li Hung Chang.

China and Russia were on the brink of a great war. The Chinese courtiers wished to fight, but Li Hung Chang longed for peace.

"Come and help me to keep peace," he said to Gordon. And "Chinese Gordon" did not fail him.

"I cannot desert China in her present crisis," he wrote.

His stay in China was not long, but when he returned to England he had made peace between two empires.

He had only been home for a short time when again he was on the wing.

One day at the War Office he met a brother officer, who complained of his bad luck at having to go and command the Engineers at such a dull place as the Island of Mauritius.

"Oh, don't worry yourself," said Gordon, "I will go for you: Mauritius is as good for me as anywhere else."

For a year he remained there—a peaceful, if dull year, but in March 1882 he was made a Major-General, and relieved from his post.

For a short time he was in South Africa, trying to put to rights affairs between the Basutos—a black race—and the Government at the Cape. The Government, who had asked him to come, treated him badly, and even put his life in danger. He made them very angry by telling them that they were wholly in the wrong, and that he would not fight the Basutos, who had right and justice on their side; and, having failed in his mission, he returned to England.

To find the rest and peace he so much needed, Gordon now went to the Holy Land.

Long ago, the day before a brave warrior was made a knight, he spent the hours from sunset till dawn alone in a chapel beside his armour, watching and praying. This was called "watching his armour."

Gordon was "watching his armour" now. Often he saw no one for weeks at a time. He prayed much, and the books he read were his Bible, his Prayer Book, Thomas à Kempis, and Marcus Aurelius. He wandered over the ground where the feet of the Master he served so well had trod before him. He was much in Jerusalem. He went to where the grey olives grow in the Garden of Gethsemane. His own Gethsemane was still to come.

In those quiet days he planned great work that he meant to do in the East End of London.

But there was other work for him to do. "We have nothing to do when the scroll of events is unrolled but to accept them as being for the best," he once wrote.

In December 1883 he suddenly returned to London, and soon it was known that he was going, at the request of the King of the Belgians, to the Congo, to help to fight the slavers there. "We will kill them in their haunts," said Gordon.

Meantime, fresh things had been happening in the Soudan.

When Gordon left Egypt in 1879, he said to an English official there: "I shall go, and you must get a man to succeed me—if you can. But I do not deny that he will want three qualifications which are seldom found together. First, he must have my iron constitution; for Khartoum is too much for any one who has not. Then, he must have my contempt for money; otherwise the people will never believe in his sincerity. Lastly, he must have my contempt for death."

Such a man was not found, and well might the black people long for the return of Gordon Pasha, the only Christian for whom they offered prayers at Mecca.

When he went away, under the rule of the greedy Egyptian pashas the slave trade began again. Once more packed caravans of wretched slaves dragged across the desert, and the land was full of misery and of rebellion.

In 1881 the discontented Soudanese found a leader.

From the island of Abbas on the Nile, Mahommed Ahmed, a dervish or holy man, from Dongola, proclaimed to the people of Egypt and of the

Soudan that he was a prophet sent from heaven to save them from the cruelty of their rulers.

El Mahdi el Muntazer, or The Expected One, he called himself, and said he was immortal and would never die.

Soon he had many followers. He was attended by soldiers, who stood in his presence with drawn swords, and he had all the power of a king. Because he was Mahdi, his followers all had to obey him. And as he was Mahdi, he himself did exactly as he pleased, and what he liked to do was all that was wicked and cruel.

The Governor-General at Khartoum, seeing that the Mahdi was growing much too powerful, sent two companies of soldiers to take him prisoner. The Mahdists made a trap for them, fell on them with their swords and short stabbing spears, and destroyed them. More troops were sent, and also destroyed. Then came a small army, and of that army almost no man escaped.

"This is in truth our Deliverer, sent from Heaven," said the wild people of the Soudan, and they flocked in tribes to join the Mahdi.

It was not long before he owned a great army, and there have never been any soldiers who fought more fiercely and with more magnificent courage, and who feared death less, than those followers of a savage dervish.

The Mahdi laid siege to one of the chief cities of the Soudan. It fell before him, and sack and massacre followed.

An army of 11,000, under the command of a brave English officer, was then sent to attack the Mahdi. Like all the troops that had gone before them, they were led into a trap, and, out of 11,000 men, only eleven returned to Egypt.

From one victory to another went the Mahdi. His troops, armed with weapons taken from those they had slain, were rich with plunder.

Only two Englishmen were now left in the Soudan. At Khartoum were Colonel Coëtlogan and Mr. Frank Power, correspondent of the *Times*.

Colonel Coëtlogan telegraphed that it was hopeless for the Egyptian troops in the Soudan to hold out against the Mahdi. Soldiers were deserting daily, and people on every hand were joining the victorious army of the ruffian who claimed to have been sent from Heaven. Colonel Coëtlogan begged for orders for the loyal troops to leave the Soudan and seek safety in Egypt.

Gordon believed that if the Soudan were given up to the Mahdi, there would presently be no limit to the tyrant's power. All the slavery and misery from which Gordon had tried to free the land would be worse than ever before. Egypt and Arabia might also, before long, take as their king the Mahdi who ruled the Soudan.

He held that at all costs Khartoum must be defended, and not handed over to the Mahdi, as Colonel Coëtlogan and many others advised.

In England this belief of General Gordon, who knew more about the Soudan than any other living man, soon became known.

All his plans for going to the Congo were made, and he had gone to Brussels to take leave of the King of the Belgians when a telegram came to him from the English Government.

"Come back to London by evening train," it said. And, leaving all his luggage behind him, Gordon went.

Next morning he interviewed Lord Wolseley and some members of the Cabinet. He was asked if he would undertake a mission to the Soudan, to try to resettle affairs there, to bring away the Egyptian garrisons, and to divide, if possible, the country amongst the petty sultans whom he thought strong and wise enough to keep order.

Gordon was ready to go, and, to go at once. "I would give my life for these poor people of the Soudan," he said.

Late that afternoon he started.

Lord Wolseley has told the story of his going:—

"There he stood, in a tall silk hat and frock coat. I offered to send him anything he wanted.

"'Don't want anything,' he said.

"'But you've got no clothes.'

"'I'll go as I am!' he said, and he meant it.

"He never had any money; he always gave it away. I know once he had £7000. It all went in the establishment of a ragged school for boys.

"I asked him if he had any cash.

"'No,' was his calm reply. 'When I left Brussels I had to borrow £25 from the King to pay my hotel bill with.'

"'Very well,' I said, 'I'll try and get you some, and meet you at the railway station with it.'

"I went round to the various clubs, and got £300 in gold. I gave the money to Colonel Stewart, who went with him: Gordon was not to be trusted with it. A week or so passed by, when I had a letter from Stewart. He said, 'You remember the £300 you gave me? When we arrived at Port Said a great crowd came out to cheer Gordon. Amongst them was an old Sheikh to whom Gordon was much attached, and who had become poor and blind. Gordon got the money, and gave the whole of it to him!'" [1]

Before he started, he gave away some trinkets and things that he prized. It was as if he knew something of what lay before him.

At Charing Cross, the Duke of Cambridge (who had known him since he was a merry little boy at Corfu), Lord Wolseley, and others, came to bid him Godspeed.

He took with him Colonel Donald Stewart, whom he had chosen as his military secretary. Even in the rush before the train started he found time to say to one of Colonel Stewart's relations: "Be sure that he will not go into any danger which I do not share, and I am sure that when I am in danger he will not be far behind."

When, on January 18, 1884, Gordon went out to the Soudan like one of the Crusaders of old, all England was proud and glad.

In Egypt the people were gladder still.

Said the Arabs who had served under him: "The Mahdi's hordes will melt away like dew, and the Pretender will be left like a small man standing alone, until he is forced to flee back to his island of Abbas."

The Khedive again made him Governor-General of the Soudan, and, on the 26th of January 1884, Gordon started for Khartoum.

At Khartoum the people were in a panic. Colonel Coëtlogan had his troops in readiness for flight. The rich people had already escaped. The poor who had not fled were in terror lest the Mahdi and his hosts might come any day and massacre them.

Across the desert spread the telegraph message: "*General Gordon is coming to Khartoum.*"

"*You are men, not women. Be not afraid; I am coming,*" followed Gordon's own message to the terrified garrison.

More swiftly than ever before, he crossed the lonely desert. Many skeletons of men and of camels, of oxen and of horses, now lay bleaching in the scorching sun on that dreary waste of treeless desolation.

On 18th February he reached Khartoum, and was greeted as their deliverer by the people, who flocked around him in hundreds, trying to kiss his hands and feet.

"I come without soldiers," he said to them, "but with God on my side, to redress the evils of the land."

At once he was ready, as in past days, to listen to tales of wrong from the poorest, and to try to set them right. He had all the whips and instruments of torture that Egyptian rulers had used piled up outside the Palace and burned. In the gaol he found two hundred men, women, and children lying in chains and in the most dismal plight. Some were innocent, many were prisoners of war. Of many their gaolers could give no reason for their being there. One woman had been imprisoned for fifteen years for a crime committed when she was a child.

Gordon had their chains struck off, and set them free. At nightfall he had a bonfire made of the prison, and men, women, and children danced round it in the red light of the flames, laughing and clapping their hands.

All the sick in the city he sent by the river down to Egypt.

In Khartoum itself, by the mercy of its Governor, peace soon reigned.

"Gordon is working wonders," was the message Mr. Power sent to England.

But the Mahdi's power was daily growing, and he feared no one. When Gordon sent him messages of peace he sent back insolent answers, calling upon Gordon to become a Mussulman, and to come and serve the Mahdi.

"If Egypt is to be quiet, the Mahdi must be smashed up," Gordon telegraphed to the English Government.

By means of his steamers he laid in stores. The defences of Khartoum he strengthened by mines and wire entanglements. He made some steamers bullet-proof, and on 24th August was able to write that they were doing "splendid work." His poor "sheep," as he called his troops, were being turned into tried soldiers. "You see," he wrote, "when you have steam on, the men can't run away, and must go into action."

Daily, from the top of a tower that he had built, he would gaze long with his glass down the river and into the country round. From there he could see if the Mahdi's armies were approaching, or if help were coming to save Khartoum and the Soudan. All the time he kept up the hearts of the people, and encouraged work at the school and everywhere else.

In his journal he wrote: "I toss up in my mind, whether, if the place is to be taken, to blow up the Palace and all in it, or else to be taken, and, with God's help, to maintain the faith, and if necessary suffer for it (which is most probable). The blowing up of the Palace is the simplest, while the other means long and weary humiliation and suffering of all sorts. I think I shall elect for the last, not from fear of death, but because the former is, in a way, taking things out of God's hands."

"Haunting the Palace are a lot of splendid hawks. I often wonder whether they are destined to pick out my eyes."

Gradually the Mahdi's forces were gathering round the city. Their drums rang in the ears of the besieged like the sound of a gathering storm. The outlying villages were besieged, and many of those villagers went over to the enemy. In some cases Gordon managed to drive back the rebels from the parts they attacked, and bring back arms and stores taken from them. More often the troops that were expected to defend Khartoum put Gordon to shame by their feebleness and cowardice, and suffered miserable defeat. Once, when attacking the Mahdists, five of Gordon's own commanders deserted, and helped to drive their own soldiers back to Khartoum.

As the year wore on, the siege came closer. Daily the Palace and the Mission House were shelled, and men were killed as they walked in the streets.

Money was scarce, and Gordon had little bank-notes made and used in place of money, so that business still went on. But food grew scarcer than money. Biscuits were the officers' chief food; dhoora that of the men.

Again and again news was sent to him: "The English are coming."

Again and again he found that the English army that was to relieve Khartoum had not yet started.

"The English are coming!" mocked the dervishes.

Day by day, Gordon's glass would sweep the steely river and the yellow sand for the first sight of the men who were coming to save him and his people.

At last, with sinking heart, he wrote: "The Government having abandoned us, we can only trust in God."

"When our provisions, which we have, at a stretch, for two months, are eaten, we must fall," wrote, to the *Times*, Frank Power, a brave man and a true friend of Gordon.

In April the telegraph wires were cut by the enemy. After that, news from England was only rarely to be had, and only through messengers who were not often to be trusted.

Still hoping that an English army was coming, Gordon determined to send his steamers half way to meet it. It meant that his garrison would be weaker, should the Mahdi make any great attack, but Gordon felt that England *could* not fail him, and that in a very short time the steamers would return, bringing a splendid reinforcement.

On September 10th, three steamers, with Colonel Stewart and Frank Power in command, sailed down the Nile.

Gordon was left the only Englishman in Khartoum.

"I am left alone ... but not alone," he wrote.

The steamer with Stewart and Power on board ran aground. The crew was treacherously taken by a native sheikh, and Stewart, Power, and almost all the others were cruelly murdered and their bodies thrown into the Nile.

The news of the death of his two friends, and the ruin of his plan to hasten on the relief of Khartoum, cut Gordon's brave heart to the quick.

Before Mr. Power left, Gordon had given him a little book that he loved. It is called *The Dream of S. Gerontius*. Gordon had marked many passages in it.

Here are some:—

> "*Pray for me, O my friends.*"
>
> "Now that the hour is come, my fear is fled ..."
> "Into thy hands
> O Lord, into Thy hands ..."

So it seemed that even then Gordon knew that Death was drawing near him, and was greeting with a fearless face the martyrdom that he was soon to endure.

Yet all the while he never wavered, and his bravery seemed to give courage to the feeblest hearted.

He who had never taken any pride in decorations or in medals—save one—tried to cheer his soldiers by having a decoration made and distributed—"three classes: gold, silver, pewter."

A Circassian in the Egyptian Service, speaking of Gordon in after years, said: "He never seemed to sleep. He was always working and looking after the people."

In the early days of those dark months, Frank Power had written of him that all day he was cheering up others, but that through the night he heard his footfall overhead, backwards and forwards, backwards and forwards, sleepless, broken in heart, bearing on his soul the burden of those he had no power to save.

At dawn he slept. All day he went the rounds, cheering up the people, seeing to the comfort of every one, feeding the starving as well as he could. For two days at a time he would go without food, that his portion might go to others. They were living on roots and herbs when the siege was done.

All the night he spent on the top of his tower, watching and praying. Many times in the day did men see the spare figure standing on that yellow-white tower, staring, with eyes that grew tired with longing, into the far-away desert, looking for the help that never came.

Looking for the help that never came

But, after many delays, an English army was actually on the march.

It was a race of about 1800 miles up the Nile from the sea—a race between Victory and the Salvation of the beleaguered city and its defender on one side, and Defeat, Death, and the Mahdi on the other.

Lord Wolseley, who commanded the expedition, offered £100 to the regiment that covered the distance first.

Some fierce battles were fought on the way, and many brave lives were lost.

On 14th December 1884, Gordon wrote to his sister: "This may be the last letter you will receive from me, for we are on our last legs, owing to the delay of the expedition. However, God rules all, and, as He will rule to His glory and our welfare, His will be done....

"I am quite happy, thank God, and, like Lawrence, I have '*tried* to do my duty.'"

On the same day he wrote in his journal:

"I have done my best for the honour of our country. Good-bye.—C. G. Gordon."

The last message of all was one that bore no date, and was smuggled out of Khartoum in a cartridge case by one who had been his servant:—

"What I have gone through I cannot describe. The Almighty God will help me."

In the camp of the Mahdi lay an Austrian prisoner, Slatin Pasha.

On the 15th of January 1885 he heard vigorous firing from Khartoum. Gordon and his garrison were preventing the Mahdists from keeping in their possession a fort which they had just taken.

In the days that followed, the firing went on, but Gordon's ammunition was nearly done, and he and his men were weak and spent with hunger.

On the night of the 25th Slatin heard "the deafening discharge of thousands of rifles and guns; this lasted for a few minutes, then only occasional shots were heard, and now all was quiet again."

He lay wide awake, wondering if this was the great attack on Khartoum that the Mahdi had always planned.

A few hours later, three black soldiers entered the prison bearing something in a bloody cloth. They threw it at the prisoner's feet, and he saw that it was the head of General Gordon.

When the relieving army reached Khartoum, they found the Mahdi's banners of black and green flaunting from its walls, and the guns that had so bravely defended it turned against them. They had come too late.

A traitor in the camp had hastened the end, and Gordon had fallen, hacked to pieces, while trying to rally his troops.

For hours after he fell, massacre and destruction went on in the city.

Fourteen years later, Lord Kitchener and his soldiers avenged that massacre, and marched into Khartoum.

The Mahdi was dead. He who boasted that he was immortal had died from poison given him by a woman whom he had cruelly used. The Mahdi's successors had fallen before a conquering English army.

When the Mahdists sacked and burned the Governor's Palace, they forgot to destroy the trees and the rose bushes that Gordon with his own hands had planted.

And in a new and lovely garden, beside a new Palace from which a brave Scottish soldier rules the Soudan, the roses grow still, fragrant and beautiful.

Khartoum is a great town now, peaceful and prosperous.

The Gordon College, where the boys of the Soudan are taught all that English schoolboys learn, is the monument that England gave to a hero. A statue of him stands in one of the squares, and to it came a poor old black woman to whom Gordon had been very kind.

"God be praised!" she cried, "Gordon Pasha has come again!"

For a whole day she sat beside the statue, longing for a look from him who had never before passed her without a friendly nod.

"Is he tired? or what is it?" she asked.

After many visits, she came home one evening quite happy.

"The Pasha has nodded his head to me!" she said.

And so, in the hearts of the people of the Soudan, Gordon Pasha still lives.

Winds carry across the desert the scent of the roses that he planted, and that drop their fragrant leaves near where his blood was shed.

And to the Eastern country for whose sake he died, and to our own land for whose honour his life was given, he has left a memory that must be like the roses—for ever fragrant, and for ever sweet.

[1] *Strand Magazine*, May 1892. By kind permission of Messrs. Newnes.

Milton Keynes UK
Ingram Content Group UK Ltd.
UKHW020826231024
450026UK00004B/417